First Facts®

Food Around the World

the **BIG** PICTURE

CAPSTONE PRESS
a capstone imprint

Sarah Levete

First Facts is published by Capstone Press, a Capstone imprint,
151 Good Counsel Drive, P.O. Box 669, Mankato, Minnesota 56002.
www.capstonepub.com

First published in 2010 by A&C Black Publishers Limited, 36 Soho Square, London W1D 3QY
www.acblack.com
Copyright © A&C Black Ltd. 2010

Produced for A&C Black by Calcium. www.calciumcreative.co.uk

042010
005769ACS11

Library of Congress Cataloging-in-Publication Data
Levete, Sarah.
  Food around the world / by Sarah Levete.
    p. cm. — (First facts, the big picture)
  Includes index.
  ISBN 978-1-4296-5539-2 (library binding)
  ISBN 978-1-4296-5540-8 (paperback)
  1. Food—Juvenile literature. 2. Food habits—Juvenile literature.
  I. Title. II. Series.

  TX355.L44 2011
  641.3—dc22   2010019987

Acknowledgements

The publishers would like to thank the following for their kind permission to reproduce their photographs:

Cover: Shutterstock: Paul Prescott (front), Kurt De Bruyn (back). **Pages:** Shutterstock: 2happy 20-21, 2009fotofriends 12-13, Bocky 2-3, 22-23, Bofotolux 6-7, Norman Chan 14-15, EtiAmmos 16-17, Fotokkden 10-11, 24, Sebastian Knight 20, Arnold John Labrentz 1, 18, Patrick Lecarpentier 10-11, Michael Ledray 4, Dmitry Naumov 4-5, Pincasso 18-19, Quayside 3, 6, Dr. Morley Read 15b, Ian Scott 13, Jose Ignacio Soto 9, Pozzo Di Borgo Thomas 17, Tomashko 21, Ingrid W 8-9, XuRa 15t, Yellowj 7, Zurijeta 14.

Contents

Our Food

Take a look at the food on your plate. Some of it probably traveled a long way before it reached you.

Planes and trains

The food you eat comes from all over the world. It is carried to stores by planes, boats, and trucks.

Where does the food you eat come from?

4

Finding food

You buy food in a store, but some people don't have stores. They eat the plants and animals where they live.

Crunch!

Fruits and Vegetables

Fruits and vegetables come in all colors and shapes. They grow in many different places.

Hot sun, cool earth

Some fruits and vegetables, such as sweet **mangoes**, grow quickly in the hot sun. Others, such as carrots, grow better under the cool earth.

Have you eaten funny-looking fruits and vegetables?

Stinging soup

Nettles grow wild in the country. You can use them to make a tasty soup—and it won't sting!

Spikey fruit!

7

Super Seed

Lots of breads and cereals are made from wheat.

Growing fast

Wheat starts as a tiny seed and grows into a tall, golden plant.

Brrum!

*Combines have huge **blades** to cut the wheat.*

Harvesttime

Wheat is cut down by **combines** when it is **ripe**. The **grain** from the wheat is made into food.

blades

9

Animals Too

Lots of food comes from animals such as chickens, goats, and sheep.

Milkshakes and more

Milk comes from cows and goats. It is used to make cheese, butter, yogurt, and cream.

Snake pie

People in different parts of the world eat different animals. Some people in cold countries eat **caribou**. In other countries people eat kangaroos or snakes.

We get most of our milk from cows.

Moooo!

Fish Food

Fish come in all shapes and sizes. People catch fish that swim in rivers, lakes, and seas.

Smells fishy

Fishing boats put the fish they catch into huge refrigerators to keep it fresh. Rotten fish smells and tastes horrible!

Fish face!

Cod is a large fish that is eaten all over the world.

Seaweed bread

Seaweed isn't just eaten by fish. You can eat pasta and bread made from seaweed.

13

Sweet Stuff

Do you know how chocolate and candy are made? They are made with some plants.

Chocolate beans

Chocolate comes from **cocoa** beans. The beans are cooked until they turn into a brown liquid—chocolate!

Yum!

Sugar juice

Sugarcane is a tall grass. The juice from the cane is boiled and cleaned. This turns it into sweet sugar.

Cocoa pods grow on cocoa trees in hot countries.

On the Farm

Some farms are like small gardens with a few animals. Other farms are huge.

Monster machines

Farmers on big farms often use huge machines such as tractors and combines.

In some countries, farmers still work without big machines.

Just enough

Farmers on small farms often grow just enough to feed their family or neighbors.

On the Move

In rich countries, people often eat food that is grown far away.

Food on the move

Lots of the food we eat is grown in hot countries. It is picked, packed, and sent to stores all over the world.

In poor countries, people usually buy food grown there.

18

Flying food

Bus and plane

Trucks carry bananas from the field to the airport. Airplanes then fly them to the countries they are sold in.

19

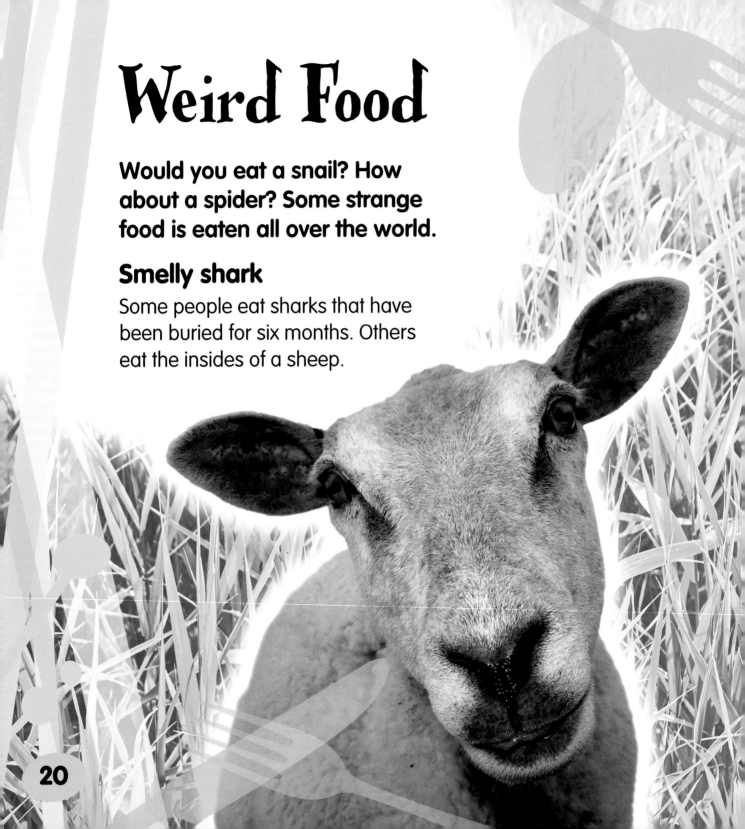

Weird Food

Would you eat a snail? How about a spider? Some strange food is eaten all over the world.

Smelly shark

Some people eat sharks that have been buried for six months. Others eat the insides of a sheep.

Tasty!

Spider snack
In some parts of the world, people eat giant crunchy spiders as a snack. Creepy!

Many people love to eat snails.

21

Glossary

blades sharp tools that can cut things

caribou animals with long horns on their heads

cereals grains that can be made into foods such as breakfast cereals, breads, and pastas

cocoa plant that contains beans from which chocolate can be made

cocoa pods part of the cocoa plant that contains cocoa beans

combines large machines that cut cereal plants when they are fully grown

grain seedlike part of a plant that is made into food

mangoes sweet, juicy fruits with an orange flesh

nettles green plants that can sting if touched

ripe when a plant is ready to be eaten

seaweed slimy plant that grows in seawater

wheat cereal plant that is made into flour for foods such as bread, cake, and pasta

Further Reading

FactHound offers a safe, fun way to find Internet sites related to this book. All of the sites on FactHound have been researched by our staff.

Here's all you do:

Visit www.facthound.com

FactHound will fetch the best sites for you!

Books

Let's Eat: What Children Eat around the World by Beatrice Hollyer (2005).

Food and The World by Julia Allen and Margaret Iggulden, Stargazer Books (2007).

Index